As dictated by The Holy Spirit
And recorded by His Unprofitable
Servant, Sam Aston Lk 17:10 KJV

Order this book online at www.trafford.com/07-2965
or email orders@trafford.com

Most Trafford titles are also available at major online book retailers.

Note for Librarians: A cataloguing record for this book is available from Library and Archives Canada at www.collectionscanada.ca/amicus/index-e.html

ISBN: 978-1-4251-6435-5

We at Trafford believe that it is the responsibility of us all, as both individuals and corporations, to make choices that are environmentally and socially sound. You, in turn, are supporting this responsible conduct each time you purchase a Trafford book, or make use of our publishing services. To find out how you are helping, please visit www.trafford.com/responsiblepublishing.html

Our mission is to efficiently provide the world's finest, most comprehensive book publishing service, enabling every author to experience success. To find out how to publish your book, your way, and have it available worldwide, visit us online at www.trafford.com/10510

www.trafford.com

North America & international
toll-free: 1 888 232 4444 (USA & Canada)
phone: 250 383 6864 • fax: 250 383 6804 • email: info@trafford.com

The United Kingdom & Europe
phone: +44 (0)1865 487 395 • local rate: 0845 230 9601
facsimile: +44 (0)1865 481 507 • email: info.uk@trafford.com

10 9 8 7 6 5 4

Table of Contents

An Explanatory Opening Note:

Actual names have purposely not been used in order to leave open the way back. God is ever dealing in hearts and lives and patiently waiting.

"... ye ought to forgive... lest perhaps such a one should be swallowed up with overmuch sorrow... Lest Satan should get an advantage of us; for we are not ignorant of his devices." 2Cor 2:7,11 KJV

The merciful Father ever waits on the returning prodigal. Lk 15:20

Win or lose, a good soldier will review the battle from hindsight to see and learn from successes or mistakes. The better be knows the enemy, the easier it will be to face him again and be successful.

To this endeavor I have been led of the Holy Spirit to relate the following events.

All verse references are from the King James Version of the Bible.

Introduction:

Assuming that you are genuinely trying to live the Christian life, then it's ultimately the Word of God you don't know that becomes Satan's greatest weapon against you!

The Spirit tells us "A little leaven leaveneth the whole lump". Gal 5:9 The right temptation draws us to sin, and from sin to more sin.

For example, we tell a "little" lie, then a "little white lie", then we must tell a blatant lie to conceal the "little" "white" lies, then... well you get the point. As the verse says the little leaven (sin) can grow to more and more sin in a downhill snowballing effect. It is true for individuals and, since individuals make up the local church, for the church as well.

Therefore, the best way to handle any recognized sin is to nip it in the bud, i.e. confess and forsake it immediately. As soon as possible, do as God teaches, "If we confess our sins

He is faithful and just to forgive us our sins, and to cleanse us from all unrighteousness". IJn 1:9

However, better is it to obey to start with. You choose to obey or disobey – even when it is not the world, or the flesh, but the devil himself who tempts you. You're responsible!

That's why we're told "... hath the Lord as great delight in burnt offerings and sacrifices, as in obeying the voice of the Lord? Behold, to obey is better than sacrifice..." ISam 15:22

So we see it pleases God greatly when we obey to start with. The reason is simple. We look like Jesus, His Son, in whom He is well pleased. Lk 3:22

Isn't that every saint's desire, to please our Heavenly Father?

Disaster often comes to a Christian because of his lack of knowledge, "My people are destroyed for lack of knowledge" Hos 4:6 It's not realizing, not considering the result of sin being contemplated that may cause us to not take sin seriously.

"Blessed is the man that walketh not in the counsel of the ungodly... but his delight is in the law of the Lord; and in His law doth he meditate day and night." Ps 1: 1-2

Obeying God's Word is our greatest weapon against Satan!

God repeatedly warns us to "know that man doth not live by bread only, but by every word that proceedeth out of the mouth of the Lord doth man live". Deut 8:3, Matt 4:4, Lk 4:4

Key to understanding His warning is to know this truth. That is, you understand it mentally and practice it in your daily life. This is to "live"; to hear and practice every word of God.

Christ, Himself, tells us, "Therefore, whosoever heareth these sayings of mine and doeth them, I will liken him unto a wise man, which built his house upon a rock; and the rain descended and the floods came, and the winds blew, and beat upon that house; and it fell not; for it was founded upon a rock". Matt 7: 24-25

The rock, of course, is Christ. He, as our savior, is our confidence, our sure footing. The it is our life built on the Savior's teaching and life example.

When we are hit hard with trials or trouble, it could be either we aren't hearing and doing (thus ignoring His warning) or we're about to have our practice catch up with our mental understanding (thus growing in grace in knowledge).

As a responsible Creator, our heavenly Father, gives the warnings because He is good. He is omniscient, and He knows what's out there – Satan and his demon followers, as well as human God and, therefore, Christian haters.

His warnings are like spiritual preventative medicine. As the secular proverb states, "forewarned is forearmed".

Few caring earthly parents can explain to young children all the possible dangers that face them in life. They must teach them what, and what not, to do until their understanding increases. In like manner God tells us to trust and obey. He warns us for our good because "He is good, for His mercy endureth forever". Ps 106:1

For this reason, to warn, with a Godly motive, He has led me to present this account of how a subtle serpent (Gen 3:1) introduced a little leaven and ruined a once successful church; my church. The devil is real! May you be forewarned. Be ready!

"I counsel thee to buy of me gold tried in the fire, that thou mayest be rich; and white raiment, that thou mayest be clothed, and that the shame of thy nakedness do not appear; and anoint thine eyes with eye salve, that thou mayest see." Rev 3:18

I

9-1-1

His tears were about to flow as my Christian brother, head down, quiet, and bewildered blurted out, half crying "I don't understand it! What's happening?"

Then the tears broke free as he wiped his eyes and complained, "It's terrible, just terrible".

I agreed, "yes, it's like a spiritual divorce". I envied him being able to cry, to have that emotional release; for I couldn't. The hurt and disgust remained within; I could not even get out a sigh.

It was after Sunday School class. Church services had preceded. We said nothing else since we had no answers; only sorrow. Going our separate ways, we drove home wondering about the outcome of the morning's events.

For over a year the church had split but the majority hadn't went anywhere – they had stayed, until now! Over half of the combined senior men's, ladies' and co-ed classes had not come to the first, traditional, worship service. The bad news was that until their requested audience with the deacons was met and resolved, abandonment of the Sunday School would soon follow.

At least some of the reason was the pulpit declaration "if you don't like me; if you don't like this church – leave!"

Many in the congregation heard, haven't been able to forget the invitation, and are obeying – they've started leaving.

At each business meeting, at each reading of the minutes, there's a list given of saints leaving; some are moving their membership, and some may leave the church altogether.

True, many visitors were coming to the contemporary, second service, and to the contemporary Sunday School. However, even their Sunday School teachers complained "many come in the front door but, just as fast, exit through the back door".

Nothing was going "right" for either group.

It's not always the cause but in answer to my prayer God reminded me "... why is thy countenance fallen? If thou doest well, shalt thou not be accepted? And if thou doest not well, sin lieth at the door...". Gen 4:6-7

The shortest verse in the Bible is "Jesus Wept". Jn 11:35

Evidentially He was allowing my Christian brother and I to see things from His point of view on that infamous day in my life that I've come to call my 9-1-1.

The sin had been introduced by the Serpent and had grown from a little thing to monstrous proportions. Now the subtle serpent made his debut as the roaring lion. IPet 5:8

The message from the pulpit has now changed to "let

us have unity", but when sin lieth at the door there can be no unity. "Can two walk together, except they be agreed?" Amos 3:3

The Devil was dancing with glee in the aisles of the Blue Sky Baptist Church!

II

In the Beginning

The Blue Sky Baptist Church as you might suspect is not the name of my church. It was the temptation offered our pastor, and through him, to the staff, to the deacons, and many of the congregation.

As one saint has said, if you want to know about now, about the future, look to the past. The Bible obviously was his basis for the teaching; "… I have somewhat against thee, because thou hast left thy first love. Remember therefore from whence thou art fallen, and repent, and do the first works, or else I will come unto thee quickly, and will remove thy candlestick out of his place, except thou repent. … He that hath an ear, let him hear what the Spirit saith unto the churches…" Rev 2:4-5, 29

I had first come here as a visitor over the July 4th holiday. Formerly I had attended a smaller Independent Baptist Church for about thirty years, i.e. since the early days of my conversion. Our pastor in his seventies, afflicted with several maladies, felt we must disband due to his inability to continue.

At his request, we prayed, agreed to disband, distributed the money in our treasury to the "front line" ministries we supported, and each person sought a new church home – one where we could continue to worship and, by His grace, to serve.

My plan was to select several churches that would possibly fit my aspirations and, by prayer and testing of the churches, go as the right church appeared.

However, as I went to my first choice, no one was there, possibly because of the Independence Day Holiday, I reasoned. So, I would be able to worship and not miss church altogether, I attended a church about three blocks away. The banner out front read "The Friendliest Church In Town". I had my doubts but it proved to be every bit of that. Bible based sermons, a good Sunday School Class, and greeters from all over led me back week after week until I realized – this is it!

True, blended music song services were entirely new to me, as were overhead projection screens in lieu of hymnals; these and the pastor was in his thirties and didn't use the old standard King James Version of the Bible.

It was a lot to consider and pray about. But God made it apparent to me that I was to stay.

After all He had a thriving church, an evangelistic outreach, Bible study and preaching from the pulpit, Sunday School fellowships, even Wednesday night meals (so people could attend and not have to worry about supper), a mother's night out program, a day care; well you get the picture although I could continue.

Recalling a former member and Sunday School teacher's question, "Why did you decide on this church?" I quickly answered I sought a place to worship and serve God. I was led here and there's been no reason to leave. He replied, "same here" with a big smile on his face.

Indeed, over the next several weeks I heard similar testimonials from all over the church and from all different age groups. Oh, there were problems (there is no perfect church), but God always seemed to work them out. His blessing was here and He was blessing!

How could it be better?

But, that's exactly the temptation waived in front of the pastor by the Deceiver:

- A traditional and contemporary service (2 distinct ones) to reach a greater audience
- A new building to accommodate the more people in Sunday School
- More Salvations
- More Ministry
- More! More! More!
- A new way to do church using the new plan for a new age

Things are changing; we must!

The Blue Sky Baptist Church is what was offered and, via the pastor's "vision", we went for it.

At least, the majority did.

Well, at first they did.

III

After the Apple

One may ask, what's bad about this, isn't growing the kingdom a good thing?

The answer is in the question; what's wrong with what we had?

The Bible tells us "Let your conversation be without covetousness, and be content with such things as ye have…". Heb 13:5

Did we not pray for what we had? Then why abandon it? If it's God's will, stay! He is the way maker and not we.

God tells what's bad about this in the example of Eli and his sons, all priests, who thought what God had given was not good enough. "Wherefore kick ye at my sacrifice and at My offering, which I have commanded in My habitation." ISam 2:29

What God had provided was not good enough any more, they wanted more. They kicked at what God had provided to represent His only Son.

Being a new member of the church, facts I did not know began unfolding one at a time; as soon as I got one down, here came another.

In a business meeting/service the pastor called for the plan to build. It apparently had been in the making for about five years.

The idea was to take a vote to receive pledges and, if the needed funds were met through the pledges, we would proceed with the building. If the funds were not pledged, we would not.

To celebrate, get everyone informed, and have everyone participate, a special off site service was held with a catered breakfast, testimonies, guest speakers and lastly the making and collection of pledges.

I still don't know how the pastor reconciled the fact that the pledges were not sufficient. He simply announced they weren't enough but he and the leadership of the church had agreed to "step out in faith" and go on with the building. Of course, all who had pledged would be held to their pledges.

Sounded real religious, I guess, "step out in faith". Wasn't that what we had already done? It seems so clear from hindsight.

If we believed God heard and answered, He said, "NO"!

Perhaps to head off controversy and resistance, he assured us that he was going nowhere, this is a we thing and not a you thing.

The sin at the door was becoming apparent. He had been given great leeway – after all he'd gotten us this far with a growing ministry. The little leaven was swelling; the pastor was out of control, but we couldn't tell it.

You may wonder, what's wrong, what's the big deal?

As one saint has said partial obedience is still disobedience.

The lie had been justified in a cloak of righteous action, but it was a mere symptom of the underlying sin that began it all.

Any means was right to obtain the Blue Sky Baptist Church.

IV

But He Didn't Roar

The pastor had told us that when we got the new plan for doing church implemented, we would kick the doors of hell in, in our community, our city and perhaps even further.

Satan was not the roaring lion we often expect, but the grinning deceiver. He had found a chink in his spiritual armor, used his leaven and was watching in delight as it worked!

It's not too wise to try to fight Satan, we're warned against it by the Spirit of God.

"Yet Michael the archangel, when contending with the devil, he disputed about the body of Moses, durst not bring against him a railing accusation, but said, The Lord rebuke thee." Jude 9

The pastor was making promises of victory but he had already been defeated.

The temptation he couldn't resist is not well recognized by saints, I'm afraid. That's how the deceiver uses it so effectively.

Yet the Holy Spirit warns us about it in the following verse.

"Mortify therefore your members which are upon the earth; fornication; uncleanness, inordinate affection, evil concupiscence, and covetousness, which is idolatry". Col3:5

Thus the Holy Spirit warns us to mortify or put to death these practices in our life. Satan seeks to resurrect them in our life.

What was his tool in our case? Inordinate affection! I can almost read some minds here; what in the world is inordinate affection? Our lack of understanding and being unable to recognize it is the reason it works against us. Perhaps now it is more understandable how a successful pastor, deacons, church leaders and church members could be duped by it.

If you don't understand God's warnings, how can the warning help you?

Just glancing at it, you might conclude INORDINATE AFFECTION is another one of those dirty, taboo, sex sins. After all it follows fornication and uncleanness. Yet it has nothing to do with sexual thoughts, speech or acts.

Possibly that's why the Spirit uses "affection', so as not to connote erotic love to the warning, but a passionate fondness.

But He alerts us to its danger with the adjective "inordinate" which means out of bounds or undisciplined. An antonym would be temperate.

Despite its' milder connotation, the Lord has said to put it to death in our lives.

An up to date example of its harm may be found in some modern homes. Many Christian parents read how to rear children according to the Bible. Chastisement is a necessary good with instructions as spare not the rod and discipline them while they are yet small. These aren't exhaustive but examples we'll use.

Yet many parents refuse to obey saying I'm not doing that to my child, for their own reasons.

When the child does wrong, they say don't do that again or I'll punish. The child tests; the parent does nothing; or at best gives one more impotent warning. You've just taught that rebellion is all right. You've just taught you're a liar and told another (the next warning) trying to support the first.

Your love is out of bounds with God's teaching.

Don't you trust Him?

"And why call ye Me, Lord, and do not the things which I say?" Lk 6:46

You can always argue to justify your action but it's always disobedience.

This principle is shown again by the following Old Testament example.

"And Nadab and Abihu, the sons of Aaron, took either of them his censer, and put fire therein, and put incense thereon, and offered strange fire before the Lord, which He commanded them not. And there went out fire from the Lord, and devoured them, and they died before the Lord." Lev 10:1-2

Aaron, Moses' brother, had two sons, priests, who were serving before the Lord for the congregation of Israel. They offered "strange fire" before the Lord and He devoured them with fire. Their sin was drunkenness as we see in verse 9 of the chapter.

"Do not drink wine nor strong drink, thou, nor thy sons with thee, when you go into the tabernacle of the congregation, lest ye die".

Many may view this as tough, perhaps overkill by the Lord. Yet we need to ask ourselves what kind of servant (minister, priest etc.) would go before "God and everybody" with such disrespect? The answer is products of inordinate affection; undisciplined sons.

Aaron's sin was his unwillingness to discipline his sons.

We see from verse 7 of the same chapter that Moses had warned Aaron against bemoaning their death or even go to their funeral. Aaron must put to death inordinate affection. He must agree with God's judgment; made because Aaron wouldn't.

"Then Moses said unto Aaron, This is that the Lord spake saying, I will be sanctified in them that come nigh Me, and before all the people I will be glorified. And Aaron held his peace." Lev 10:3

Now! Aaron displayed the discipline of God, His teaching, His presence, and, above all, to obey in front of and as an example to the congregation.

Our pastor should have said, we didn't get the required pledges; God said, "No"! Blessed be the name of the Lord; we asked; He answered; He is good! This was the time to mortify (put to death) inordinate affection.

God gives us warnings with a compassionate motive.

Suppose He did not act just as Aaron did not act. People could, and many probably would, reason if it's all right for a man of God to act like this, it's alright for us. Just offer any old sacrifice in any fashion – God will graciously accept us. Live as you please, for if you can minister drunk, you can do anything, right?

"The wages of sin is death." Has not changed. Rom 6:23a

And yet this may be only the preliminary result of such sin.

Today parents may say if I discipline my child, they could report me at school. I could go to jail. I could earn the reputation of a child abuser.

A person can justify not obeying God, but it will only get worse, maybe even death. Then death may bring the unthinkable... You know that there's a hereafter! Lack of discipline may be instrumental to your child being judged at the Great White Throne.

Recognize it! Inordinate affection is a very serious sin.

V

What's happening?

By the time we saw the events of 9-1-1 happen, it was after a little inordinate affection had grown to such proportions that the lion, Satan, was roaring – but few understood why.

Our pastor had been following God, God had blessed, our church was reaching out, people were being saved, baptisms were common, and the devil couldn't stand it.

After the decision to go ahead anyway with the building of the church and implementing the new better way; to get everyone involved in ministry and save more people, God was still saying "No"! The pulpit thinking seemed to be if we build it, He'll bless it. But, people were growing more dissatisfied with the plan.

The first service, the traditional, suffered more and more.

The music service was only a skeleton of what it had been and, according to computer buffs among us, sermons were coming straight off the internet and had no Spirit in them anymore. Rumors, gossip and confrontations became more and more prevalent.

Loss of members equated to loss of offerings and therefore to poor financial conditions.

God was speaking to us, in His silence! The leadership evidentially thought God was testing our faith and commitment. People were beginning to attribute the works of Satan to God.

Was it because God could not help us against such a foe as Satan?

"Behold, the Lord's hand is not shortened, that it cannot save; neither His ear heavy; that it cannot hear." Is 59:1

No! It was because God would not hear. He created hard love!

"But your iniquities have separated between you and your God, and your sins have hid His face from you, that He will not hear." Is 59:2

The only help was to obey "Mortify... inordinate affection". Now pride was added to the lie, that was a result of disobedience and had a firm hold on the Pastor's inordinate affection for the Blue Sky Baptist Church.

Was the plan that promised it evil? Actually it had a very good record of use by others. It proposed the methods and teaching for success but it also contained warnings. Warnings that consisted of existing conditions – that if they were present, could easily end in disaster if the plan was followed. The temptation was too great; the pastor ignored the warnings; the disasters came and he still could not let go.

Of this inability, God has given us another example in the Old Testament. Inordinate affection can involve people and we found it can also involve an idea or concept such as the Blue Sky Baptist Church. But the Holy Spirit won't accept it. He clearly has told us to put to death inordinate affection.

For God will not allow another to replace Him. In Exodus 20:5 we read "Thou shall not bow down thyself to them, nor serve them, for I the Lord thy God am a jealous God..." Just as a husband or wife cannot tolerate their spouse to share them with another, even more, God.

"if any man come to Me, and hate not his father and mother, and wife, and children, and brethren, and sisters, yea, and his own life also, he cannot be My disciple", was a quote from Christ in Luke 14:26.

In I Sam 2:11 we see a priest named Eli who was trusted as a man of God to rear and teach Samuel the prophet when Samuel was still a child.

"And Elkanah (Samuel's father) went to Ramah to his house. And the child (Samuel) ministered to the Lord before Eli the priest."

However there was a problem. "Now the sons of Eli were sons of Belial (the devil); they knew not the Lord". ISam 2:12

But the sons were allowed to serve, and sent their servant in service to the people offering sacrifices.

"And if any man said unto him (the servant), let them not fail to burn the fat presently, and then take as much as thy soul desireth; then he would answer him, Nay, but thou shalt give it me now, and if not, I will take it by force. Wherefore the sin of the young men was very great before the Lord; <u>for men abhorred the offering of the Lord</u>". ISam 2:16-17

Obviously Eli was disciplining Samuel but not his own sons. Things got worse.

"Now Eli was very old, and heard all that his sons did unto all Israel; and how they lay with the women that assembled at the door of the tabernacle of the congregation" ISam 2:22

How could Eli allow this, as a Godly priest serving God in the temple where God came to meet His people? Along with Aaron, Eli fell to his inordinate affection.

In ISam 2:23-25 we see Eli telling them don't do it any more, you're priests. He's and old man now and his lack of discipline over the years caused the warning to go ignored once more.

God would wait no longer. He sent a man of God to Eli in ISam 2:27 and in verse 29 he charges Eli; "Whereforce kick ye at My sacrifice and at Mine offering, which I have commanded in My habitation AND THOU HONOREST THY SONS ABOVE ME..."

This is a great sin, this inordinate affection.

"Of how much sorer punishment, suppose ye, shall he be thought worthy, who hath trodden under foot the Son of God, and hath counted the blood of the covenant, where with He was sanctified, an unholy thing, and hath done despite unto the Spirit of grace?" Heb 10:29

Eli's undisciplined, out of bounds love for his evil sons leads to their deaths, Eli's and his sons, in ISam 2:31,34.

Not only this result, but also, the hurt to the people came from Eli's sin.

"... And the Word of the Lord was precious (rare), in those days there was no open vision" ISam 3:1

The priesthood had failed. No wonder then that God called Samuel to be a prophet though he had been trained as a priest!

VI

The Revelation

No one seemed to know what was happening to our church by now. Due to the financial crunch, a decision was made to drop day care. Open disgust and criticism broke out in the meeting announcing the decision. Along with the loss of outreach this ministry provided, we lost more members – never to return. Three associate pastors had left during this time and were replaced with two new ones.

Nothing would get in the way of the new plan, though it was sinking. In fact, that was behind the answer a deacon had sought from me about the cause of our situation. I told him it was similar to a pilot of a great ship, our pastor; he had deliberately driven it into a storm; he had then lost control of it; and he was unable to regain it. It proved to be a better explanation than anyone else had at the time.

The pastor stopped Sunday night services because the preparing of a traditional and a contemporary service drained him. He said he just couldn't do it.

As a result, a group of seniors sought and got permission to teach a prophecy lesson. It would be on a weekday night that would not interfere with the Wednesday night services.

It became quite a success with visitors from other churches coming to it. Such a success that it brought trouble.

According to the study leaders, the pastor purposefully failed to put the study in the church bulletin. He moved the place they met from week to week and at least once didn't provide a key to gain entrance to the church so attendees could get in.

The pastor's undisciplined affection for the new plan, led to envy, deceit, perhaps hatred. Lord help us was my (and I'm sure many others) constant prayer. He evidently had mercy and let us in on what was happening.

Not by accident our Sunday School was studying the last chapter of II Samuel. When I read it, it was a total puzzle to me but, under the guide of the Spirit, I was to learn it was an example of our dilemma.

Usually, the Sunday School commentaries help with problem areas, but neither they nor the three other commentaries I had could help me.

I started preparing for it on Monday night to be taught the following Sunday. I was getting nowhere in my allotted study time so I decided to retire for the evening.

Like the prophet Samuel, ISam 3,

I was kept awake by the Spirit. He began reminding me

of the text I had just put down and then calling to my memory verses explaining it. I'd get one cleared up, get up from bed, turn on the light, write it down and say thanks and lie down. Then He'd do the same for the next verse; I'd get up again etc. This process went on from about 10:30 pm to midnight. At the end of it all, I was never more aware of God speaking to me in all of my life.

How amazing that He'd bless me with understanding that five commentators couldn't help me with.

Not until I presented it to our full Sunday School of women, men and co-ed classes did I really see it as an answer to our current situation.

At the end of the teaching, one of our leaders was visibly shaken as the assembly was dismissed. I had seen that kind of conviction before but I didn't know why here and at this time. I was to find out why shortly.

For, within days, I was invited to a dinner/discussion over concerns with our church. The group was making an in-depth study of the new way of doing church; to use for charges of wrong doing against the pastor. There were more meetings and more studying but I was under conviction not to attend any more. This was the beginning of spiritual divorce, a split. God hasn't changed His assessment of such activities.

"For the Lord God of Israel, saith that He <u>hateth</u> putting away." Mal 2:16

Obviously, the group had shaken off the Spirit's conviction from last Sunday. One of the group said they had talked with the pastor; the pastor had made promises, and then didn't keep them.

I didn't know the solution but I did know God doesn't

need any help with chastisement.

"I will be his father, and he shall be my son, If he commit iniquity, I will chasten him with the rod of men." 2Sam 7:14

This time the dissenting group planned to present the deacons with a list of findings from their search of the new church plan. They'd let the deacons consider their allegations, and then meet with the deacons and ask the pastor to answer their charges.

God still hates divorce!

Their solution was to get rid of the pastor or we go. The ball was in the deacon's hands.

VII

The Bloody Eye and Broken Tooth

How grateful I was for God's revelation to me from His Word as to what was going on. And even more so, that, though the other members wouldn't hear, God had allowed me to show His position.

The problem didn't go away and, though I understood, God was not through with His message.

I became under heavy conviction to speak to the pastor, but my reasoning kept getting in the way. Surely some one else would be better qualified; perhaps one better acquainted with him. God wouldn't let me have my way; I'd asked for wisdom about the matter; He'd given it but, as Moses, I asked, "Who am I that I should go". Ex 3:11

Then I began doubting my reasoning because the problems between the pastor, the accusing members, and the deacon committee got worse. I'd done my best to stay out of it largely because I couldn't see how I could be in the middle and be right. But because of the growing gravity of the situation, I seriously sought God's help to allow me to see is this my reluctance to obey or am I a victim of my own ego? That's what I'd been telling myself.

What an embarrassment; out of nowhere it seemed; I developed a large blood spot in the bottom half of my right eye. Everyone at work noticed it as well as people at church and my family, but I had no answer for it.

At least, not at first. A fellow saint told me 'it may be from an allergy'. She had seen it happen to others and the allergy had been the culprit. Thus, I used medicated eye drops and the problem cleared up shortly.

Could this be God's answer or perhaps just coincidence? Either way I thought if God did want me to approach the pastor, the best way would be personal correspondence, not before a committee or the church staff or office personnel, not in front of anyone.

Only days later, I found myself listening to my dentist. He was amazed that, by eating a soft cookie chased by milk, I had broken off a molar even with the gum line. A pricey restoration was in order.

As I drove home from the dentist, I said, "God I wanted to see", thanks. I'm slow but I get it. The bloody ugly red eye is how You see our situation; and as the broken tooth needed immediate attention, so did the problem at hand.

The letter I wrote was essentially a repeat of the Sunday

School lesson. It wasn't just for my benefit in order to teach, not even also for our Sunday School class, but also for the pastor.

"Who am I"? The one God gave the understanding and the task.

VIII

The Letter

For good understanding let me say, the letter, as you might suspect, had as its theme Inordinate Affection. It was king David's second infamous sin. Let's look at some background. "And Absalom spake unto his brother Amnon neither good or bad; for Absalom hated Amnon, because he had forced his sister Tamar. And it came to pass after two full years..." 2 Sam 13:22-23a

A son of David's, Amnon, had raped his half sister Tamar; Tamar's brother Absalom wanted justice; verse 21 tells us David was mad but after 2 years, David, as father and king, did nothing. So Absalom did!

"Now Absalom had commanded his servants, saying mark yet now when Amnon's heart is merry with wine, and when I say unto you, <u>smite Amnon</u>; then <u>kill</u> him..." 2Sam 13:28

David was again grieved, now with a raped daughter, a dead rapist son, and another son a killer.

"So Absalom fled, and went to Geshur and was there 3 years; and the soul of king David longed to go forth unto Absalom, for he was comforted concerning Amnon, seeing he was dead". 2Sam 13:38-39

Inability to discipline was David's problem. No punishment, he just wished they hadn't done it. Why do anything to Absalom, it won't bring Amnon back anymore than punishing Amnon would have undone Tamar's rape.

David's love for his sons, perhaps all of his children, was unregulated by obedience to God's Word.

Had these men not been his own sons, their punishment would have been quick and decisive. He was a bloody man, a man of war, a king and a father.

But instead of decisive judgment, two years went by in Amnon's case, three years went by in Absalom's case but no justice, no discipline came forth.

David's inaction spoke at least as loud as his actions to his children, his people, and his fighting men.

He had an Achilles heel, a chink in his spiritual armor, and Satan had discovered it; Inordinate Affection.

From the account given in the following verses, we see Absalom grows worse and David still does nothing.

"Absalom said moreover, Oh that I were made a judge in the land, then every man which hath any suit of cause might come unto me, and I would do him justice! And it was so, that when any man came nigh to him to do him obeisance, he put forth his hand, and took him, and kissed him. And on this manner did Absalom to all Israel that came to the king for judgment, so Absalom stole the hearts of the men of Israel". 2Sam 15:4-6

Absalom promised justice, which David did not deliver. He plotted against his father to take the kingdom.

2 Samuel 15:7 relates this went on for 40 years! Could we possibly be so gullible as to think David did not know what Absalom was doing? Could David's subjects not know? Inordinate affection has no cure, no help, as God has said it must be put to death. Col 3:5

Then Absalom makes his move. "But Absalom sent spies throughout all the tribes of Israel saying, As soon as ye hear the sound of the trumpet, then ye shall say Absalom reigneth... and the conspiracy was strong; for the people increased continually with Absalom". 2Sam 15:10, 12b

Since David won't obey God, and won't kill his son, he runs for now he has no other choice. He runs from both.

"And David said unto all his servants that were with him at Jerusalem, Arise, and let us flee, for we shall not escape from Absalom.." 2Sam 15:14

Finally, under the relentless pursuit of Absalom, David's army made a stand against Absalom's.

"So the people went out into the field against Israel; and the battle was in the wood of Ephraim" 2Sam 18:6

Civil war had begun.

"Where the people of Israel were slain before the servants of David, and there was a great slaughter that day of 20,000 men." 2Sam 18:7

David had instructed his men not to harm Absalom, but David's general disregarded his orders. 2 Sam 18:7

"... And he took three darts in his hand, and thrust them through the heart of Absalom, while he was yet alive in the midst of the oak". 2Sam 18:14

But the king had no care for his servants who died for him but only sympathy for his rogue son.

"And the king was much moved, and went up to the chamber over the gate, and wept: and as he went, thus he said, O my son Absalom, my son, my son, Absalom, would God I had died for thee, O Absalom, my son, my son!" 2Sam 18:33

The wages of inordinate affection is death. You may not mortify it, but, if not, it will make you wish you had.

IX

The Consequence of Sin

So out of line was David's affection for Absalom, that his general, Joab, reprimanded him saying "... I perceive that if Absalom had lived, and all we had died this day it had pleased thee well". 2Sam 19:6b

"... and all the people came before the king for Israel had fled everyman to his tent. And all the people were at strife throughout all the tribes of Israel..." 2Sam 19:8b-9a

Ten tribes of Israel had made Absalom King, choosing him over David because of his lack of leadership concerning his son. After the battle, there remained strife; Israel had to be talked into recognizing the king for they fled to their tents after the battle.

As David returned home, strife broke out again between the ten tribes that had followed Absalom and the two tribes that had remained loyal to David.

"And the men of Israel answered the men of Judah, and said, we have ten parts in the king and we have also more right in David than ye; why then did ye despise us, that our advice should not be first had in bringing back the king? <u>And the words of the men of Judah were fiercer than the words of the men of Israel</u>." 2Sam 19:43

Satan had them against each other and was keeping them there.

Then among David's own followers, rebellion breaks out.

"And there happened to be there a man of Belial, whose name was Sheba, the son of Bichri, a Benjamite; and he blew a trumpet, and said, We have no part in David, neither have we inheritance in the sons of Jesse, every man to his tents, O Israel". 2 Sam 20:1

"So every man of Israel went up from after David; but the men of Judah clave unto the king, from Jordan even to Jerusalem". 2Sam 20:2

David sent his army and put down the rebellion by killing Sheba.

David then engages in combat with his old previously defeated enemies as they flare up again. He is able to quell them.

But the unrest in his kingdom persists. They had chose Absalom and though he had been defeated did not want God's man "... We will not have this man to reign over us." Lk 19:14

Though God was handling David's chastisement, the

people did not want His repentant King.

While the unrest and discontent with the king was boiling we read the Destroyer's working. "And Satan stood up against Israel, and provoked David to number Israel". I Chron 21:1

After David's judgment, i.e. the death of Absalom, and forgiveness of Israel's mutiny by not retaliating and accepting them back; Israel only saw it as more weakness and refused God's anointed.

The Devil was holding them back using David's failure for reason not to return.

Then Satan turns to David, who had forgiven the ten tribes and paid for his sin, and provokes David to take a count of just who is on my side and who isn't.

David's fed up with their disloyalty and unforgiveness and calls for a yea and nay vote. "And again the anger of the Lord was kindled against Israel, and he (Satan from IChron 21:1) moved David against them to say, Go number Israel and Judah". 2Sam 24:1

As a result, God kills seven thousand men by His angel, seen as a pestilence by the people according to 2Sam 24:15.

David realizes the deaths are his fault, he's responsible as leader, as king, as father for failure to rule under the Lord's guidance.

"And David spake unto the Lord when he saw the angel that smote the pople, and said, Lo, I have sinned, and I have done wickedly; but these sheep, what have they done? Let Thine hand, I pray Thee, be against me and against my father's house". 2Sam 24:17

God accepts a burnt offering sacrifice and David is forgiven. "And David built there an alter unto the Lord, and offered burnt offerings and peace offerings, so the Lord was entreated for the land and the plague was stayed from Israel." 2Sam 24:25

Had God not acted, the nation would have split, maybe even self destructed, and we would have had no savior, for Christ's linage was from David.

X

After giving the background and interpreting the study, I continued to relate to the pastor how it all applied to what was happening at our church.

It was the reason for the tremendous dissention, contention, distrust and, yes, even hate within the "fellowship" of believers.

By example or type the pastor was the cause of it initially. His inordinate affection for Absalom. Satan had made a new application in the use of an old device.

Instead of involving people as in Aaron, Eli, and David's cases, the masquerading angel of light used a concept.

Pastor you are David and your Blue Sky Baptist Church is Absalom. I didn't use my name for his idol but the new plan he had used to model after. I believe he read it all. The Holy Spirit had not let me walk away from teaching it to the Sunday School class nor writing it to the pastor.

Therefore, I'm confident He made sure the pastor understood it, even if somehow I had not written it clearly. His promise is that His word never returns void. Is 55:11

Even if it was to a pastor, the solution was simple. As David the pastor needed to say those three hardest words to utter, I HAVE SINNED!

I had written the letter by hand as soon as I got home that evening. I was considering typing it and putting it in better order, but the Spirit impressed on me the urgency to send it now.

Putting my street shoes and clothes on, I drove to the local post office and mailed the letter.

Whatever ensued I had peace that I was doing God's will; I prayed the pastor would also. I didn't know if he'd answer at all, or, if he did, would seek to put me in my place as a mere layman having the audacity to call a seminary trained pastor into account.

To my delight, he did call me at my office the next day and asked to have lunch with me to discuss the letter. After more prayer I was looking forward to the meeting with high expectation. God was working.

While eating and discussing the letter and circumstances that faced him and the church, I couldn't help noticing I was eating but he was not. He said he'd not had much appetite lately. Obviously sitting and waiting on the deacon council's decision had him uneasy. I'd hoped it was also due to God's conviction of the truth of the letter.

I got to the point as quickly as I could asking him if he

had read the letter and if he understood what I had written. He said he did and that I had confronted him the right way i.e. one on one rather than in front of the deacon council. He said he couldn't understand the ones making the charges. They acted as though he had committed some unforgivable sex sin like adultery or something.

I went back to the letter and reminded him about his new church implementing two services. Jesus warned us "a house divided against itself cannot stand". Matt 12:25

At that, he answered BUT and my great expectations began to wane. For I'd met the nasty little three letter word before while teaching Sunday School.

The pastor said yes he heard and understood what I was saying. BUT you haven't heard my side of it. It wasn't for me to hear and decide, only to tell.

Apparently he felt I had listened to the "other side" and had sided with them. I told him, "I'm only trying to tell you God's word to me for you". My personal position is that neither "side" is right in this, and, therefore, God is not pleased with any of us.

He didn't seem to accept my reply. He said he thought he could reconcile matters if the leader of the dissenters would only meet with him one on one as we had done. Then I was told his real motive for our meeting. He asked me to arrange a meeting between them. The sad reasoning was "they respect you, maybe they'll agree".

Reluctantly, I agreed. Then again, perhaps this was to be God's plan to reconcile the whole hopeless affair. The word BUT had me down; I couldn't forget it.

I hadn't wanted to get involved at all but, I certainly have no better solution, so I'll do it as unto the Lord, relying on

His word "blessed is the peacemaker".

That night I phoned the leader and told him the whole account of God's using the Sunday School lesson in 2 Samuel as an example of our dilemma; even about the bloody eye and the broken tooth. Being as honest as I knew how, I tried to make sure both parties had the same information.

He may laugh, I thought, and call me hopelessly fanatical, but I'd depend on God's impressing the account.

We had passed from 2 Samuel to the study of Ephesisans in Sunday School. I reminded him about the teaching of obeying the Holy Spirit's guide and the request of the pastor was presented.

Then I was hit below the belt. He said, "I know we're grieving the Holy Spirit" Ep4:30, But!

As the pastor, he heard, he understood, BUT I'm going my way. He related how he had talked to the pastor one on one already and the pastor lied to him. Whatever happened to the seventy times seven rule, I thought. Evidently, not wanting to go further with the conversation, he said to tell the pastor that, "you and I tried that; it didn't work; it's up to the deacons and their decision now, and that's how it's going to stay".

The pastor had said, if you don't like me or this church, LEAVE!

The accusing group was saying it's my way or the highway! Jesus wept still!

The deacon council gave its answer; they backed the pastor; and their reply was see you in heaven. I don't know the council's motives for the decision, but I hope it was made by conviction of the Holy Spirit.

The dissenters left.

And just as David's count for who was on his side turned into a body count, so the pastor was to experience his.

Many had already left as mentioned previously. Many more were to follow.

Of those who stayed that went to the traditional service, many came to Sunday School only and either went to another church for the worship service, or just went home.

Thus the early service was reduced to a mere token of what it had been, with a lacking music service and messages from the pastor that those in attendance doubted. In their eyes he had stolen their church.

To no one's surprise, the first service was dropped hoping attendees would join in the second contemporary service. But the split had occurred, some staying and some leaving, and what remained became an even greater problem.

XI

The Hereling

As Eli, the pastor had remained unrepentant. He refused to mortify his inordinate affection for the Blue Sky Church.

We were all finding out that when God says thus saith the Lord, He means it. His NO is NO!

Ministries had no funds to do ministry; they were reduced to meetings. This brought on disillusionment in the new program, it wasn't working. Money was scarcer than ever. The leadership became worried that the church's witness would be hurt due to it's inability to pay it's debts. Staff paychecks were late and held until the offerings were such to release them. Tempers mounted as worries over paying for the great debt for the new building grew. More people left.

I suppose in a desperate attempt to get the church back to worship instead of worry, the pastor started a new Bible study on Wednesday evenings in the Gospel of John. He had been preaching topical messages on Sunday mornings. The last study, in Revelation, he did not finish, I'm thinking because of all the problems within our congregation.

As he progressed in John, some people in the class asked questions he didn't answer, probably fearing their doubt of his ability.

To others he reminded them he knew the Greek language so as to say I'm right so don't worry about what else it might mean. I struggled along with this until he got to Chapter 10 and he began to teach about the Good Shepherd.

In verse 12 and 13 he quite noticeably pronounced hireling as hereling. Fearing I was on the verge of becoming just another preacher basher, I kept quiet, but, I didn't forget the obvious mispronunciation.

"I am the Good Shpherd; the Good Shepherd giveth His life for the sheep; But he that is a hireling, and not the shepherd, whose own the sheep are not, seeth the wolf coming, and leaveth the sheep, and fleeth; and the wolf catcheth them, and scattereth the sheep. The hireling fleeth, because he is an hireling and careth not for the sheep". Jn 10: 11-13

The pastor had a college degree from a very good secular college and a master's degree from a prominent seminary. He had to know the difference between hereling, as he pronounced it, and hireling as it was written.

Looking from hindsight, I believe he was being convicted by the Holy Spirit whle he was speaking and, consciously, purposefully, chose hereling. Maybe it occurred to him that some of the members might put two and two together.

For not long after, he announced to the congregation on Sunday morning that he had accepted a pastorate in another church in a distant state. He told us it was not a snap decision. We knew he had been visiting at least one other church and, according to him, the one he was going to had been working with him for over six months.

I'm sure many, as I did, remembered his promise to the church as he led us to accept the new way of doing church, the needed new building, more parking and the two Sunday morning services. "We're in it together; you don't have to worry about me; I'm not going anywhere."

God was removing him and his unruly son, the Blue Sky Baptist Church.

No one said it but I believe many members were saying to themselves, how could this pastor now expect an offering and bon voyage fellowship dinner to help him and his family start at his new pastorate? That's what he did and it was granted to him! His audacity truly confounded me. I really didn't want to go and I knew it. To say the least, the pastor was a great disappointment, like a captain leaving a sinking ship, only me first. But the problem really was I needed to use IJn 1:9. After confessing my sinful thoughts, God revealed all the right reasons not to attend.

I could attend; I could help with the money, I could join in with the others and wish him well, but God convicted me not to do so. What would the others think? I'd be a villain in their eyes. But each time I prayed over my objections God impressed upon me the harder that I was not to be a participant.

I agreed with Him and then He reminded me of a teaching of His which gave me a reason for the way He was leading me. I realize that, when God tells me to obey, He may not tell me why, but I thanked Him for doing so in this case.

In IKings 12:26-28a we see, "And Jeroboam said in his heart, Now shall the kingdom return to the house of David; If this people go up to do sacrifice in the house of the Lord at Jerusalem... Whereupon the king took counsel, and made two calves of gold, and said unto them... behold thy gods...".

The nation of Israel had split. In order to maintain his kingdom in the north, Jeroboam, institutes idolatry.

As a result God sends an unnamed prophet to warn the king. "And behold, there came a man of God out of Judah by the word of the Lord unto Bethel; and Jereboam stood by the altar to burn incense. And he cried against the altar in the Word of the Lord..." IKi 13:1,2a

After delivering his message, the prophet was asked by the king "...come home with me and refresh thyself, and I will give thee a reward." IKi 13:7

In reply the prophet answers, "...It was charged me by the Word of the Lord, saying, eat no bread, nor drink water, nor turn again by the same way that thou camest". IKi 13:9

The point was that, after delivering a message of warning, if the prophet then had fellowship with the one warned, the prophet would nullify God's word. It would be as if the king said all right, you did what you think is God's will, I can respect that. You've done what you had to; let's put it behind us. We're all just saved sinners, right?

God had told the prophet don't do it! In just such a manner I understood that, having the privilege of being God's spokesman to the pastor, I could cancel God's message He'd given though me.

Furthermore, I was not only not to participate and simply avoid the pastor; I was not to go at all!

In IKings 13 the prophet is tricked by one of Satan's, he lied telling him God had changed His mind and it was now all right to have fellowship with the lying prophet. IKi 13:18

God's prophet made a mistake. He disobeyed the known will of the Lord. "So he went back with him..." IKi 13:19

"And when he was gone, a lion met him by the way and slew him..." IKi 13:24

Thus I saw if I went to the bon voyage for the pastor, even though I avoided him, it would be construed as my wishing him Godspeed. As I was representing God's Word it would be like saying God changed His mind.

But, He hadn't.

I could not go at all.

Else I'd fall victim to the lion, a type of the devil I believe, who wanted me to fail as God's messenger by compromising the force of the word God was using in the pastor's heart.

I stayed home that evening. I prayed for him that he might yet hear God and turn and then I prayed for our church, for its future.

I still pray for him as often as the Spirit reminds me. Probably not for what he wants, but I ask for God's will in his life.

Hopefully, he'll find his way back and not be put on a shelf forever.

"But I keep under my body, and bring it into subjection; lest that by any means, when I have preached to others, I myself should be a castaway." I Cor 9:27

But, as far as I know, he has not returned to God as David did. Therefore, like Eli, God ended His ministry through the pastor; at least at our church.

XII

Beauty For Ashes

My outlook changed immediately, for I knew God was working in our midst. My prayer became the psalmist's, "I have gone astray like a lost sheep, seek thy servant" Ps 119:176

My prayer for our church was like that for an individual. Our church was sheep that had gone astray. Only God could help.

Now the ruins of inordinate affection, the remnant of our church had no shepherd, little money to pay one, and no sure direction at the moment. God had removed the problem, now we were solely dependent on Him. It's exactly where He wanted us, "...and He will dwell with them, and they shall be His people and God Himself shall be with them, and be their God..." Rev 21:3b

Satan had had his heyday but the God of all grace, the Good Shepherd, had come for us.

Our problems didn't go away all at once. Satan did not want us to rebuild, to again be of service to the Lord, and a light in our part of this dark world.

Satan hates resurrection! The Spirit tells us "for the builders, every one had his sword girded by his side, and so builded. And he that sounded the trumpet was by me." Neh 4:18

The verse refers to how the returning exiled Israelites rebuilt Jerusalem after their captivity in Babylon.

Israel's enemies didn't want the wall, the temple and the city rebuilt.

"When Sanballat the Horonite, and Tobiah the servant, the Amonite, heard of it, it grieved them exceedingly that there was come a man to seek the welfare of the children of Israel." Neh 2:10

For the Israelites to rebuild, they had to be ready to defend themselves with their swords handy. They were aware of their enemies' cunning and also kept a watchman with a trumpet on lookout at all times.

Just so, our church would need to rebuild as Israel; with the Word (our sword) handy at all time, and paying heed to the watchman (the Holy Spirit) as he warns of possible enemy attacks.

The devil is a formidable foe. He's relentless in his objective. "And when the devil had ended all the temptation, he departed from Jesus <u>for a season</u>". Lk 4:13

The Holy Spirit warns us he'll be back. Stay alert; be sober; he's looking for a gap in your spiritual armor. IPet 5:8

Pray for us to heed God's warnings. Gal 6:2

Pray for you and your church as well. I Cor 10:11-12

"From whence come wars and fighting among you? Come they not hence, even of your lusts that war in your members? ...Submit yourselves therefore to God. Resist the devil, and he will flee from you. Draw nigh to God and He will draw nigh to you." James 4:1, 7-8

For about a year after the pastor left, we had interim supply pastors on Sunday mornings, while staff and deacons filled in at other services.

We had some bumps along the road as we went, turmoil still flared up now and then, but the leadership drew nearer to God.

He already had a pastor for us; one was in the "wings" of the church, an associate. Like Samuel in the Old Testament was being trained for when Eli was removed, so the associate was being prepared of God to replace our former pastor. He already knew our position and had initially said no but realized God's will for him.

We needed a specific Shepard just for us; one with a care for us as God had. He's proved to be a model of the good shepherd, willing to invest his life in us.

Almost immediately, he began warning us Satan was real, we needed to be aware of him, and be prepared for him.

A new building fund campaign has been implemented and has thus far been a success.

He emphasizes the need for daily devotion, Bible reading and prayer. He himself is our example to hide the word in our heart's that we may not sin against God.

Pray for our pastor. 2Th5:23-25

Pray for your own. ITim2:1-2

Could your pastor, your church be duped by the deceiver? Perhaps with the last temptation you might be able to think of, the old serpent could do it again.

How could it work?

None of us saw what he tempted us with. All "sides" held the "other" side at fault and he was unidentified for the most part as the problem.

Why not take a little inordinate affection, wrap it in a religious plan formulated to kick the doors of hell in and call it the Blue Sky Baptist Church?

Let us praise God for His precious promises.

But, let us likewise praise Him for His gracious warnings. "Mortify therefore your members which are upon the earth; fornication, uncleanness, inordinate affection, evil concupiscence, and covetousness, which is idolatry". Col3:5

"He that hath an ear, let him hear what the Spirit saith unto the churches". Rev 2:29

So true are the words of the hymn.

"Trust and Obey,
For There's No Other Way,
To be Happy in Jesus,
But to Trust and Obey."

How simple is life when we obey but how complicated it becomes if we do not.

Forgiveness, mercy and grace are much less needed for the obedient. But, after experiencing the loss of Eden, I find myself identifying with Adam, indebted to our Great God of mercy, forgiveness and grace!

www.ingramcontent.com/pod-product-compliance
Ingram Content Group UK Ltd.
Pitfield, Milton Keynes, MK11 3LW, UK
UKHW020136250726
13967UKWH00002B/689

9 781425 164355